Animal Trivia
Questions

Written by Simon Tudhope

Illustrated by Sarah Horne

Designed by Kate Rimmer

Big cats

1. Which is the only big cat that hunts in groups?

2. Which big cat has the largest population and lives in the most countries?

   a) cheetah   b) cougar   c) leopard

3. Jaguar comes from a Native American word meaning what?

   a) 'He who kills with one leap'
   b) 'He who kills with his feet'
   c) 'He who kills many sheep'

4. Is the bushy hair on a male lion's head called a mane or a mullet?

5. From how far away can you hear a lion's roar?

   a) 1.5km (1 mile)
   b) 8km (5 miles)
   c) 16km (10 miles)

(6) **Fill in the blanks with either 'J' for jaguar or 'L' for leopard.**

... climbs trees to eat or sleep.

... has the strongest bite of any big cat.

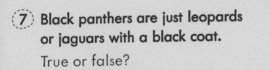

(7) **Black panthers are just leopards or jaguars with a black coat.**

True or false?

(8) **In Roman gladiator shows, lions and tigers were pitted against each other.**

Which cat won most of the fights?

(9) **In the Bible story, who was thrown into a lions' den?**

a) David   b) Duncan   c) Daniel

(10) **I'm from the hot grasslands in Africa. I have a tassel on the end of my tail. I'm known as the king of the beasts.**

What am I?

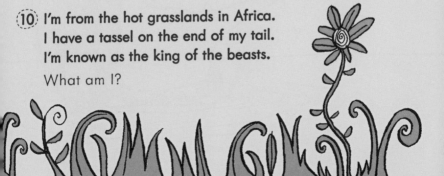

Definitely deadly

1. **Which of these animals kills the most people?**
   a) lions   b) sharks   c) hippos

2. **Which bird plucks monkeys out of the trees to eat?**
   a) king vulture   b) fearful owl   c) harpy eagle

3. **Which shark can live in rivers?**
   a) whale shark
   b) bull shark
   c) great white shark

4. **What African animal is nicknamed the laughing assassin?**

5. **On average, how many people are eaten by crocodiles each year?**
   a) 100   b) 1,000   c) 5,000

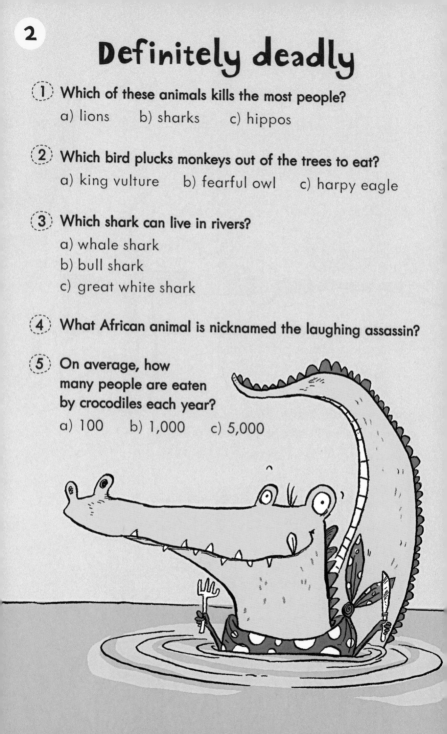

6 **What is the world's most venomous animal?**
   a) box jellyfish
   b) king cobra
   c) funnel-web spider

7 **What small fish from the Amazon river can bite your finger off with one snip?**

8 **Which deadly mythical beast has only one eye?**
   a) cyclops
   b) werewolf
   c) basilisk

9 **Where could you be stung by a box jellyfish, munched by a saltwater crocodile and bitten by a black widow spider?**
   a) Spain   b) Greece   c) Australia

10 **Which dangerous snake might you come across in the desert?**
   a) sidewinding adder
   b) boa constrictor
   c) green mamba

11 Which animal has the most powerful bite in the world?
  a) grizzly bear   b) crocodile   c) great white shark

12 Which creature causes more human deaths than any other on the planet?

13 What is the only animal that can drive a wolf pack off its territory?

14 How do anaconda snakes kill their prey?
  a) biting   b) squeezing   c) stinging

15 How should you deal with a charging rhino?
  a) keep quiet and throw a rock to one side
  b) shout and scream as loudly as you can
  c) punch it on the nose

Sharks

1) After a big meal, how long can a great white shark go without eating?

   a) 2 days
   b) 2 weeks
   c) 2 months

2) Sharks have very sensitive electrical sensors. What do they use them for?

   a) to detect their prey's movements
   b) to communicate with each other
   c) to avoid boats and submarines

3) Which would win in a fight between a great white shark and a killer whale?

4) What would happen if you turned a shark upside down?

   a) it would drown
   b) it would fall into a trance
   c) it would swim around in circles

5) What is the name of this shark?

6 In 2007, sharks killed one human. How many sharks did humans kill in the same year?

   a) 1 million   b) 10 million   c) 100 million

7 Sharks swim in their sleep, otherwise they'd:

   a) sink   b) drown   c) be washed ashore

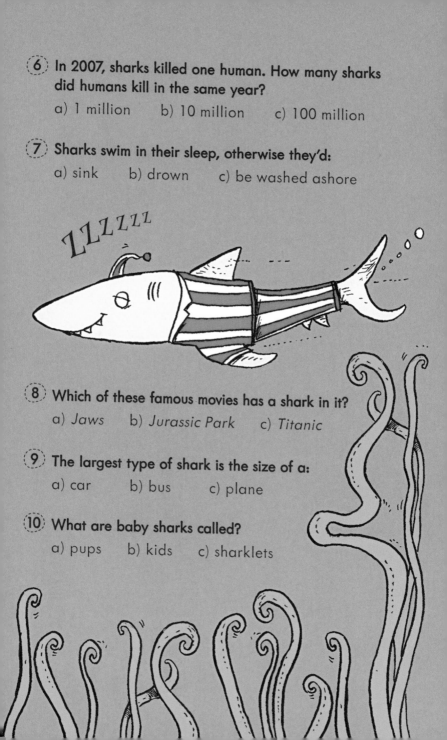

8 Which of these famous movies has a shark in it?

   a) *Jaws*   b) *Jurassic Park*   c) *Titanic*

9 The largest type of shark is the size of a:

   a) car   b) bus   c) plane

10 What are baby sharks called?

   a) pups   b) kids   c) sharklets

Forest dwellers

(1) Which country has
the most wolves?
a) Canada
b) Russia
c) United States

(2) I have a bushy tail...
...and black and white fur.
I defend myself with a foul spray.
What am I?

(3) Which farm animals are wild
boars most closely related to?
a) cows   b) sheep   c) pigs

(4) Foxes living in snowy forests
have what type of fur?
a) red   b) white   c) black

(5) Do squirrels live in nests?

AWOOOO

(6) **Dogs are most closely related to which forest animal?**
   a) wolves
   b) foxes
   c) badgers

(7) **What are baby porcupines called?**
   a) porcupups
   b) porcupettes
   c) porcupops

(8) **I have two big front teeth...**
   ...and a talent for felling trees.
   I'm also Canada's national animal.
   What am I?

(9) **How fast can a woodpecker peck wood?**
   a) 6 times per second
   b) 16 times per second
   c) 160 times per second

(10) **Which animal hibernates in winter?**
   a) hedgehog   b) pigeon   c) cat

11. In the book by Jack London, what type of forest animal was White Fang?

12. Do bears like honey?

13. Whose Grandma lived in a forest and was eaten by a wolf?
    a) Snow White
    b) Humpty Dumpty
    c) Little Red Riding Hood

14. What do roe, red and fallow have in common?

15. Where do Siberian tigers live?
    a) Scandinavia
    b) Alaska
    c) Russia

Pets

1. If a cat falls, does it always land on its feet?

2. Which is the most popular pet worldwide?
   a) dog b) cat c) fish

3. What should be the main part of a house rabbit's diet?
   a) carrots
   b) hay
   c) lettuce

4. What's the name of Dennis the Menace's pet dog?
   a) Chomper b) Snarler c) Gnasher

5. All cats are born with blue eyes.
   True or false?

6 Which is smaller:
a hamster or a guinea pig?

7 What was the name of the dog that rode on a Soviet spacecraft in 1957?
a) Laika   b) Pushkin   c) Lenin

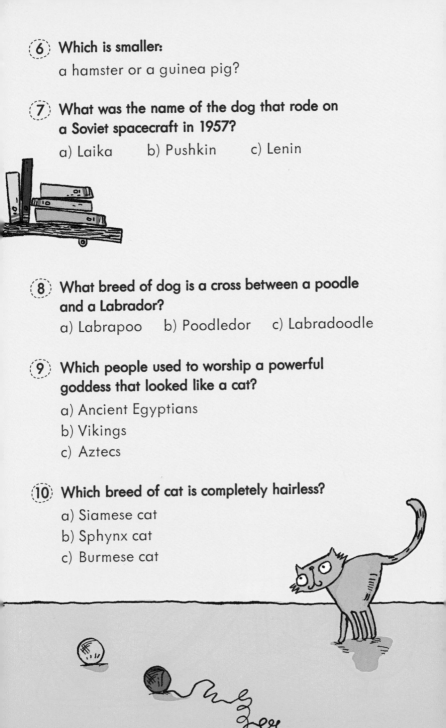

8 What breed of dog is a cross between a poodle and a Labrador?
a) Labrapoo   b) Poodledor   c) Labradoodle

9 Which people used to worship a powerful goddess that looked like a cat?
a) Ancient Egyptians
b) Vikings
c) Aztecs

10 Which breed of cat is completely hairless?
a) Siamese cat
b) Sphynx cat
c) Burmese cat

11 What type of pet did miners once take down the mines to test the air safety?

a) dog   b) goldfish   c) canary

12 Is it true that goldfish have a three-second memory?

13 What is the name of the Simpsons' pet dog?

a) Santa's Little Helper
b) Snowball
c) Stompy

14 Do rabbits thump their back legs on the ground to warn other rabbits of danger, or to start a courtship dance?

15 How far can a hamster run in one night?

a) 0.6km (1 mile)
b) 30km (20 miles)
c) 100km (60 miles)

Monkeys and apes

1. Which type of primate lives only on the island of Madagascar?
   a) orangutan
   b) lemur
   c) rhesus monkey

2. What is a group of monkeys called?
   a) pack   b) tribe   c) troop

3. What is the legendary ape that's said to walk on two legs and live in the forests of North America?
   a) King Kong   b) Bigfoot   c) Yeti

4. Does a proboscis monkey have:
   a) a giant nose?
   b) a fat belly?
   c) a huge moustache?

5. No wild monkeys live in Europe.
   True or false?

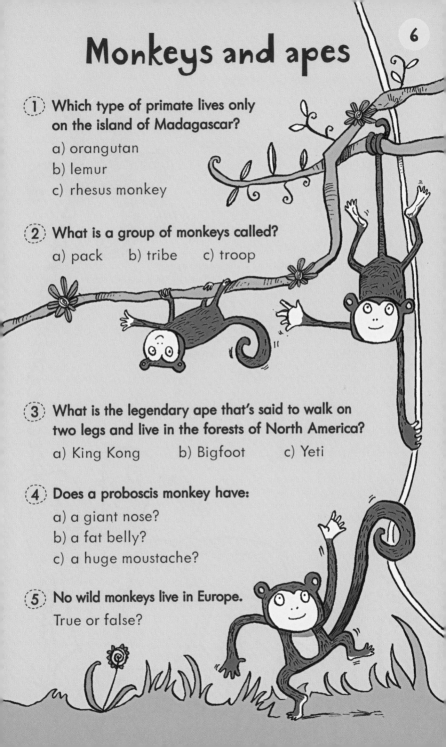

6 **What's the quickest way to tell a monkey from an ape?**

7 **Which is the largest type of ape?**
   a) gorilla
   b) orangutan
   c) chimpanzee

8 **Which monkey escapes the winter chill by bathing in hot springs?**
   a) mandrill   b) capuchin   c) Japanese macaque

9 **How did Ham the chimp make history in 1961?**
   a) he was the first ape to release a pop song
   b) he was the first ape in space
   c) he was the first ape to do long division

10 **What's the name for an adult male gorilla?**
   a) silverbull
   b) silverback
   c) silverking

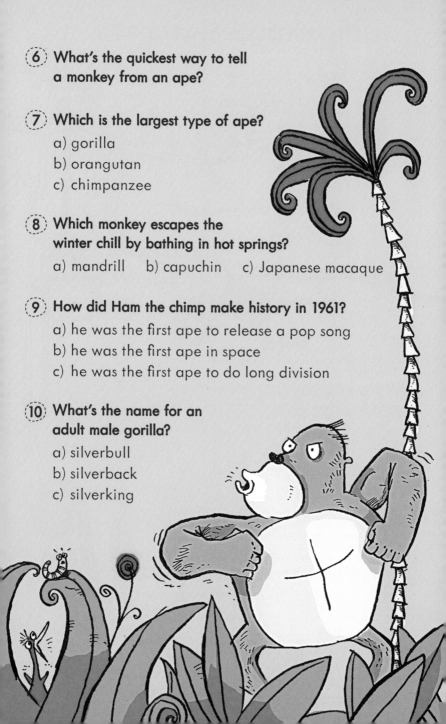

Animal giants

1) **Which of these is a nickname for a giraffe?**
   a) stench pig   b) reek hog   c) stink bull

2) **What is the largest animal that's ever lived?**

3) **Which large, flightless bird defends itself with a dagger-like claw on each foot?**
   a) emu   b) cassowary   c) ostrich

4) **How does a little bird called an Egyptian plover help Nile crocodiles?**
   a) it pecks their skin clean of tiny pests
   b) it warns them of danger
   c) it cleans their teeth

5) **What's the name of the giant Japanese movie monster that has atomic breath?**

6 Which of these big animals could you NOT see in the forests of eastern Russia?

a) tigers
b) bears
c) gorillas

7 In China, are dragons said to bring good luck or bad luck?

8 Crocodiles were around at the same time as the dinosaurs.

True or false?

9 In Roald Dahl's book, what is the BFG?

a) a big friendly giraffe
b) a big friendly giant
c) a big friendly gorilla

10 A blue whale's heart is the same size as a:

a) beachball
b) washing machine
c) car

11. 'Orca' is another name for which animal?
    a) killer whale   b) elephant   c) python

12. Which animal has the largest eyes in the world?
    a) blue whale   b) colossal squid   c) whale shark

13. Which big, bad-tempered animal has a hide
    that's so thick it's almost bulletproof?
    a) hippo   b) buffalo   c) tiger

14. Did cavemen ride woolly mammoths?

15. Put these animals
    in order of size,
    largest first.
    a) sperm whale
    b) dolphin
    c) leopard
    d) hippo

Birds of prey

1. Which birds of prey are usually bigger: males or females?

2. I can turn my head nearly all the way around. I see ten times better than humans at night. I fly in almost total silence.
   What am I?

3. Which of these kills other birds in the air?
   a) peregrine falcon
   b) sea eagle
   c) snowy owl

4. What is the name of an eagle's nest?

5. What are a bird of prey's feet called?
   a) claws
   b) talons
   c) pincers

6. Are vultures hunters or scavengers?

7. Which of these is not a bird of prey?
   a) buzzard   b) gannet   c) kestrel

8. Secretary birds stand over 1m (3ft) tall and stalk through grasslands looking for prey.
   Where do they live?
   a) Africa   b) Asia   c) Australia

9. In the *Harry Potter* books, what is the name of Harry's owl?
   a) Scabbers   b) Hedwig   c) Pig

10. Which of these is most likely to be seen in Europe?
    a) golden eagle   b) bald eagle   c) harpy eagle

Creepy-crawlies

1) **How many legs do spiders have?**
   a) 6   b) 8   c) 10

2) **Which creatures eat meat:**
   millipedes or centipedes?

3) **How did Spiderman get his superpowers?**
   a) he was bitten by a radioactive spider
   b) he swallowed a radioactive spider
   c) his parents were spiders

4) **I have eight legs.**
   I have large pincers and sting with my tail.
   My deadliest species is called 'deathstalker'.
   What am I?

5) **What do head lice feed on?**
   a) hair
   b) blood
   c) dry skin

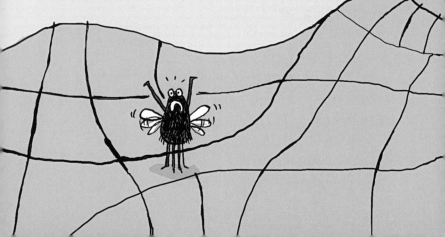

6. Do bed bugs bite?

7. What's often used by fishermen as bait?
   a) slugs
   b) beetles
   c) maggots

8. Which is the largest spider in the world?
   a) Goliath bird-eating spider
   b) wolf spider
   c) king baboon spider

9. Do millipedes have a venomous bite?

10. 0.5kg (1lb) of spider thread
    would wrap around:
    a) an athletics track
    b) New York City
    c) the Earth

11) Amazonian giant centipedes are the length of your:
   a) finger
   b) hand
   c) forearm

12) Can spiders climb up through the drain in a bathtub?

13) All centipedes have 100 legs.
   True or false?

14) Stick insects are made of wood.
   True or false?

15) If you cut an earthworm in half, do you get two live worms?

Yes or no?

1. Do gorillas build nests?

2. Do toads lay toadspawn?

3. Could a blue whale swallow a person?

4. Could a polar bear swim across the English Channel?

5. If a homing pigeon brings you a message, can you send it back with a reply?

6. Do giraffes have more neck bones than people?

7. Can a dolphin recognize itself in a mirror?

8. Can tigers swim?

9. Do turtles sweat?

10 Are all four feet of a galloping horse ever off the ground at the same time?

11 Are slow worms slower than earthworms?

12 If a cow falls over, can it get back up?

13 Does a jellyfish have a brain?

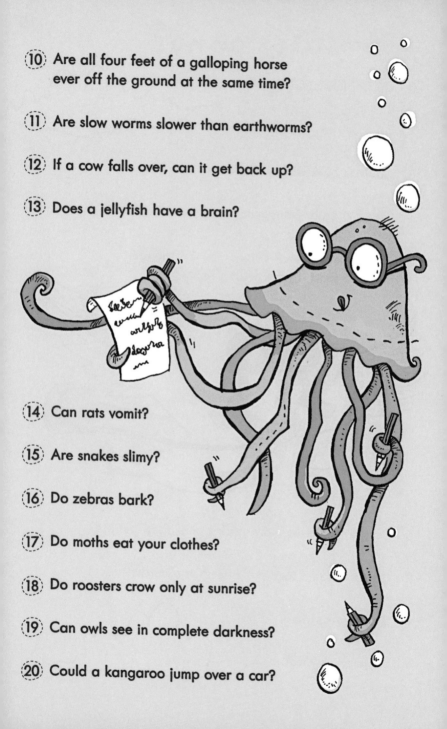

14 Can rats vomit?

15 Are snakes slimy?

16 Do zebras bark?

17 Do moths eat your clothes?

18 Do roosters crow only at sunrise?

19 Can owls see in complete darkness?

20 Could a kangaroo jump over a car?

On the farm

1) **What were the very first farm animals?**

   a) goats   b) sheep   c) pigs

2) **Which is the most intelligent?**

   a) horse   b) pig   c) chicken

3) **Only female chickens lay eggs.**

   True or false?

4) **What are Holsteins, Friesians, Jerseys and Guernseys?**

5) **What is a horse's size measured in?**

   a) hands   b) arms   c) legs

6) **What is a group of geese called?**
   a) giggle   b) gaggle   c) goggle

7) **Which animal has a comb and wattle?**
   a) cow
   b) pig
   c) chicken

8) **Do cows always lie down when it rains?**

9) **What do you call a male goat?**

10) **Roughly how many times do cows pass gas each day?**
   a) 15   b) 150   c) 1,500

Snakes

1. **What part of their prey do spitting cobras target?**

   a) eyes   b) nostrils   c) mouth

2. **What is the longest snake in the world?**

   a) fer de lance
   b) reticulated python
   c) boa constrictor

3. **In which of these places do snakes not live?**

   rainforests, deserts, polar regions, oceans, grasslands

4. **Which snakes are normally used by snake charmers?**

   a) adders   b) mambas   c) cobras

5. **Do snakes have bones?**

6 Which mythical character had snakes for hair?

a) Medusa   b) Minotaur   c) Cerberus

7 How do desert snakes move across the sand?

a) slithering   b) side-winding   c) rolling

8 Which of these countries has no native snakes?

England, France, Ireland, Italy

9 According to tests, which land snake has the most toxic venom in the world?

a) spitting cobra   b) coral snake   c) inland taipan

10 Can rattlesnakes hear their own rattle?

Fish

1 Which is the odd one out?

tuna, swordfish, pike, barracuda, mackerel

2 Which movie had two clownfish in starring roles?
a) *The Little Mermaid*
b) *Finding Nemo*
c) *Shark Tale*

3 What do fish breathe through?
a) gills b) nostrils c) skin

4 Are starfish really fish?

5 Where did goldfish originally come from?
a) Italy b) Brazil c) China

(6) Which fish is said to have the most painful venom of any animal in the world?

a) puffer fish   b) stonefish   c) catfish

(7) A salmon lays about 3,000 eggs at a time. Roughly how many will reach adulthood?

a) 2   b) 100   c) 1,500

(8) You can catch a trout by gently tickling its belly.

True or false?

(9) The sea captain in the Tintin books is called Captain Haddock.

True or false?

(10) How long can a flying fish glide above water?

a) 10 seconds
b) 20 seconds
c) 40 seconds

Bears

1. **Which bear is vegetarian?**
   a) grizzly bear   b) black bear   c) giant panda

2. **What was the name of the bear in *The Jungle Book*?**
   a) Baboo   b) Baloo   c) Bagoo

3. **Are koalas a type of bear?**

4. **Where can you see the Great Bear and the Little Bear?**

5. **What type of fish do grizzly bears catch in summer?**
   a) salmon
   b) tuna
   c) cod

6 Which bear is very good at climbing trees?

    a) black bear   b) polar bear   c) grizzly bear

7 What did Winnie the Pooh and Piglet try to trap in a deep hole with a jar of honey?

    a) a womble

    b) a moomin

    c) a heffalump

8 When it's hunting in the ice and snow, a polar bear covers its black nose to blend in with its surroundings.

    True or false?

9 What makes up 80% of a grizzly bear's diet?

    a) meat

    b) fish

    c) plants

10 *Ursus maritimus* is the scientific name for which bear?

    a) polar bear

    b) brown bear

    c) panda

11) In California in the 1850s, cage fights were held between grizzly bears and lions.
Who won?

12) What do polar bears never eat?
   a) penguins   b) seals   c) fish

13) Which of these is a real bear?
   a) bearded bear
   b) spectacled bear
   c) gloved bear

14) Who stole the three bears' porridge?
   a) Pinocchio
   b) Little Bo Peep
   c) Goldilocks

15) Why do pandas do handstands?
   a) to scent-mark a tree
   b) to impress a mate
   c) to exercise

The seasons

1. What letter shape do a flock of geese form when they migrate?

2. Why don't you see wasps in winter?
   a) they're hibernating
   b) they migrate
   c) they're nearly all dead

3. Every year, 1.5 million wildebeest, gazelles and zebras trek northward through southern Africa. This huge annual migration is nicknamed:

   'The Greatest _____
   on _____.'

4. Is a stoat in its white winter coat called an ermine or a moomin?

5. What's the name of the hard case that protects a caterpillar as it changes into a butterfly?
   a) chrysalis
   b) carapace
   c) kernel

6) Do any animals that live near the equator hibernate?

7) Where do European barn swallows spend winter?
   a) Australia   b) Africa   c) Asia

8) Which of these animals changes its coat in winter?
   a) Arctic fox   b) wolf   c) polar bear

9) Do all birds migrate?

10) When squirrels store nuts for the winter, do they bury them separately, or in a large stash?

In the desert

1. **Which camel has two humps:**
   Bactrian or Dromedary?

2. **How do dancing white lady spiders get out of trouble?**
   a) by leaping up and down very quickly
   b) by burrowing into the sand
   c) by cartwheeling down a sand dune

3. **Which beetle did the Ancient Egyptians worship?**
   a) scarab beetle
   b) stag beetle
   c) elephant beetle

4. **A dust devil is a type of lizard that runs so fast it sends clouds of dust into the air.**
   True or false?

5. **How long can a camel go without drinking?**
   a) 4 days
   b) 4 weeks
   c) 4 months

6 What do horned lizards squirt from their eyes?

    a) tears   b) saliva   c) blood

7 Why do shovel-snouted lizards dance?

    a) to keep their feet cool
    b) to attract a mate
    c) to confuse predators

8 What's the name for a group of camels that are transporting goods?

    a) wagon   b) caravan   c) fleet

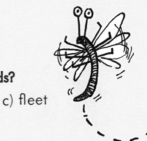

9 Which lizard rolls up into a spiky coil to defend itself?

    a) armadillo lizard
    b) anteater lizard
    c) aardvark lizard

10 Do scorpions sting with their tail, their pincers or both?

Defensive trickery

1. This fish inflates to look larger than it really is. Is it called a:

   a) porcupine fish?
   b) balloon fish?
   c) gulper fish?

2. Which African ant-eating animal can somersault away from danger?

   a) aardvark   b) honey badger   c) meerkat

3. Which of these animals does NOT blend in with its surroundings?

   a) tiger   b) chameleon   c) poison-dart frog

4. Why do baby komodo dragons roll themselves in dung?

5. How do geckos distract a predator?

   a) by releasing a smelly gas
   b) by doing somersaults
   c) by discarding their tail

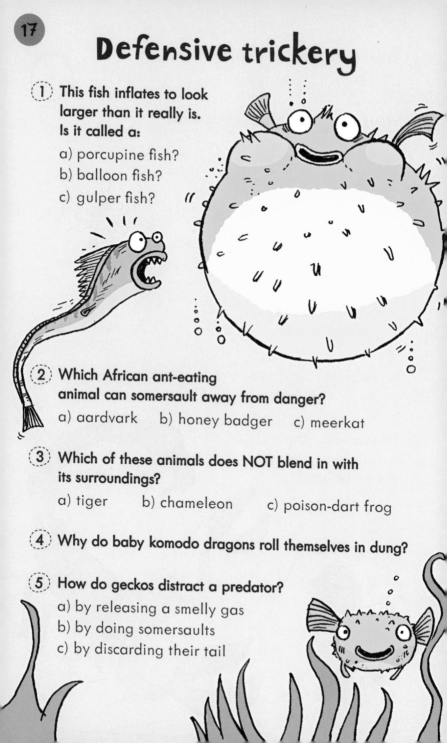

6 Which animal plays dead, and inspired the phrase:
"playing p_ _ _ _m"

7 Which grumpy desert animals burp up semi-digested food and spit it at whatever's annoying them?

8 There's a fish that has two pupils in each eye, to help check for predators. One looks above the water, and one looks below.

What is its common name?
four-_ _ _ _ fish

9 What does a skunk's spray smell most like?
a) rotten eggs and rancid milk
b) burning rubber and urine
c) dog mess and sweat

10 Which animal rolls into a ball, like a hedgehog?
a) armadillo
b) porcupine
c) koala

Down under

1. What's the name for animals that carry their babies in a pouch?

2. I live on an island near Australia.
   I have extremely strong jaws.
   My cartoon character spins like a tornado.
   What am I?

3. What is a baby kangaroo called?
   a) bunny   b) sheila   c) joey

4. What's the name of Australia's jackal-like predator?
   a) dingo   b) quango   c) mungo

5. There are only two egg-laying mammals in the world. One is the platypus, what is the other?
   a) echidna   b) numbat   c) bandicoot

6 How many hours
do koalas sleep a day?

   a) 5 hours
   b) 10 hours
   c) 20 hours

7 Do wombats live in nests or burrows?

8 Which Australian spider eats her
male partner after mating?

   a) pirate spider
   b) black widow spider
   c) trapdoor spider

9 What kind of animal is a kookaburra?

   a) bush rabbit   b) bird   c) squirrel

10 All marsupials come from Australasia.
True or false?

Myth or fact?

1. Ostriches bury their heads in the sand.

2. Flamingos stand on one leg.

3. Elephants are scared of mice.

4. Crocodiles cry.

5. Kangaroos box.

6. Lemmings jump over cliffs.

7. Camels store water in their humps.

8. Only female mosquitoes bite.

9. Baby chicks touched by a human are abandoned by their mothers.

10. Bird's nest soup is made from birds' nests.

11 Starfish can grow a whole new body from one arm.

12 Mongooses are immune to snake venom.

13 Crabs walk sideways.

14 Bats are blind.

15 Lions can't purr.

16 Dogs see in black and white.

17 You can hear the sea inside a shell.

18 Daddy long-legs are venomous.

19 Earwigs live inside your ear.

20 Bloodhounds have the best sense of smell of any dog.

Seashore

1. **Which of these animals often live in rockpools?**
   crabs, starfish, seahorses, limpets, herrings

2. **Which bird dives head-first into the sea to catch fish?**
   a) osprey   b) herring gull   c) gannet

3. **Are Australian swans black, white or brown?**

4. **What do octopuses squirt to drive away predators?**
   a) milk   b) ink   c) blood

5. **Which type of crab looks for an old shell to live in?**

HOME SWEET HOME

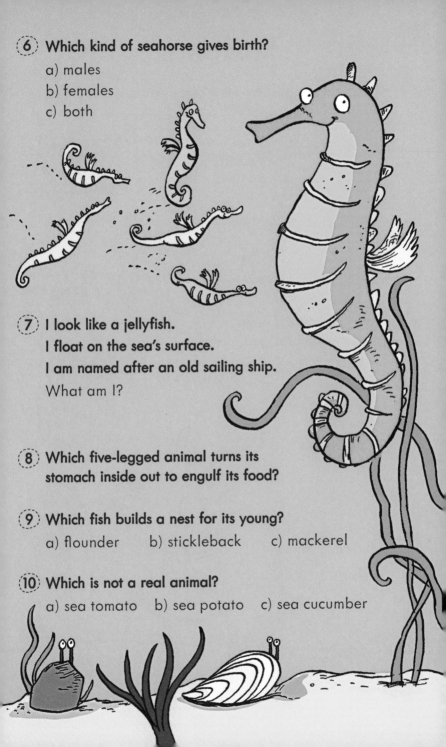

6) **Which kind of seahorse gives birth?**
   a) males
   b) females
   c) both

7) I look like a jellyfish.
   I float on the sea's surface.
   I am named after an old sailing ship.
   What am I?

8) **Which five-legged animal turns its stomach inside out to engulf its food?**

9) **Which fish builds a nest for its young?**
   a) flounder   b) stickleback   c) mackerel

10) **Which is not a real animal?**
    a) sea tomato   b) sea potato   c) sea cucumber

Rodents

1. The world's largest rodent is a capybara. It's as big as a:
   a) cat　　　b) sheep　　　c) donkey

2. What were Alvin, Simon and Theodore?
   a) mice　　b) squirrels　　c) chipmunks

3. From how great a height could a mouse fall and survive?
   a) the roof of a house
   b) the top of a crane
   c) a cruising jumbo jet

4. Do squirrels hibernate?

5. How many grandchildren could a female rat have?
   a) 15
   b) 150
   c) 1,500

6 Which type of rodent carried fleas that brought the Black Death plague to medieval Europe?

a) harvest mouse   b) black rat   c) shrew

7 House mice can squeeze through cracks the width of a:

a) raspberry   b) strawberry   c) plum

8 In the story of the Pied Piper of Hamelin, which animals were lured away by the piper's music?

9 Which of these is not a rodent?

a) lemur   b) beaver   c) gopher

10 Are porcupines related to hedgehogs?

Ends of the Earth

1. Is a polar bear's skin:
   a) black?   b) white?   c) pink?

2. I live in large colonies.
   I look like a gigantic brown slug...
   ...with 1m (3ft) long tusks.
   What am I?

3. Do penguins live near the
   North Pole or the South Pole?

4. What type of dogs pull snow sleds?
   a) Labradors   b) Alsatians   c) huskies

5. While looking after its egg,
   how long does an emperor
   penguin go without eating?
   a) 2 days
   b) 2 weeks
   c) 2 months

6 How far can polar bears swim without stopping?
  a) 3km (2 miles)
  b) 80km (50 miles)
  c) 650km (400 miles)

7 Which of these are reindeer belonging to Santa?
  Dasher, Ranger, Prince, Comet, Clanger, Blitzen

8 Can seals sleep in the sea?

9 Which of these doesn't live in the Arctic or Antarctic?
  wolverine, snow leopard, seal, musk ox, snowy owl

10 Arctic terns migrate from the Arctic to the Antarctic
  and back again. How far is the round-trip?
  a) 2,500km (1,500 miles)
  b) 75,000km (45,000 miles)
  c) 120,000km (95,000 miles)

Lizards

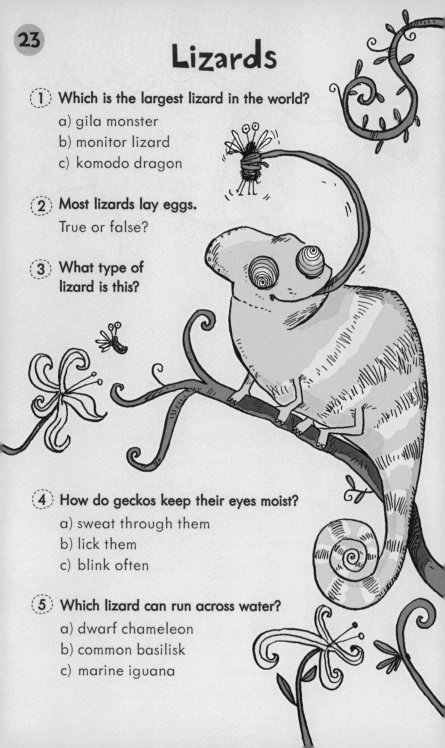

① **Which is the largest lizard in the world?**
   a) gila monster
   b) monitor lizard
   c) komodo dragon

② **Most lizards lay eggs.**
True or false?

③ **What type of lizard is this?**

④ **How do geckos keep their eyes moist?**
   a) sweat through them
   b) lick them
   c) blink often

⑤ **Which lizard can run across water?**
   a) dwarf chameleon
   b) common basilisk
   c) marine iguana

(6) **Which lizard can walk across ceilings?**
   a) monitor lizard
   b) iguana
   c) gecko

(7) **Which statement about komodo dragons is false?**
   a) they spit acid
   b) they eat their own babies
   c) they have a venomous bite

(8) **How can you tell a legless lizard from a snake?**
   a) lizards have no scales
   b) lizards have ear holes
   c) legless lizards don't slither

(9) **Are lizards warm blooded or cold blooded?**

(10) **Only one of these is a lizard. Which one?**
   a) earthworm   b) hookworm   c) blindworm

Frogs and toads

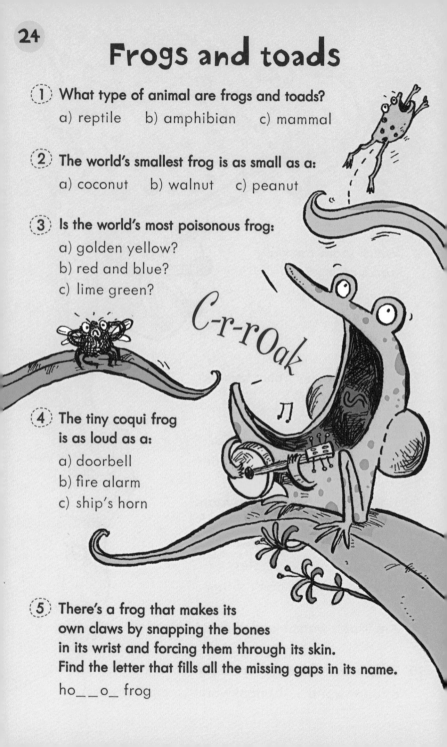

1. **What type of animal are frogs and toads?**
   a) reptile   b) amphibian   c) mammal

2. **The world's smallest frog is as small as a:**
   a) coconut   b) walnut   c) peanut

3. **Is the world's most poisonous frog:**
   a) golden yellow?
   b) red and blue?
   c) lime green?

4. **The tiny coqui frog is as loud as a:**
   a) doorbell
   b) fire alarm
   c) ship's horn

5. **There's a frog that makes its own claws by snapping the bones in its wrist and forcing them through its skin. Find the letter that fills all the missing gaps in its name.**

   ho_ _o_ frog

6 Do frogs have teeth?

7 Why does a frog pull its eyeballs into its head?
   a) to disguise itself as a leaf
   b) to protect them when under attack
   c) to help push food down its throat

8 Which toad was brought to Australia to eat a plague of sugar-eating beetles, but has multiplied and spread uncontrollably?
   a) cane toad   b) natterjack toad   c) bush toad

9 In *The Muppet Show*, which frog is Miss Piggy in love with?
   a) Fozzie the frog
   b) Kermit the frog
   c) Gonzo the frog

10 Toads give you warts.
   True or false?

After dark

1) Match each tawny owl with its call:
   - a) male
   - b) female
   - 1) tu-whit
   - 2) tu-whoo

Tu-whOOoo

2) Which night animal is the most common predator on the planet?

3) Which insect looks like a dull type of butterfly and flies at night?

Tu-Whit

4) Do foxes hibernate?

5) Which animal are badgers most closely related to?
   - a) bear
   - b) weasel
   - c) rat

6) I am plain and brown.
I have a beautiful voice, and often sing at night.
I share my name with a famous nurse.
What am I?

7) What sound do hedgehogs make?
a) snort   b) bark   c) purr

8) Which animal completes this verse
by William Blake?
'_____ _____ burning bright,
in the forests of the night.'

9) Moles are only active at night.
True or false?

10) What type of creature is this?
a gopher or a tarsier?

Bats

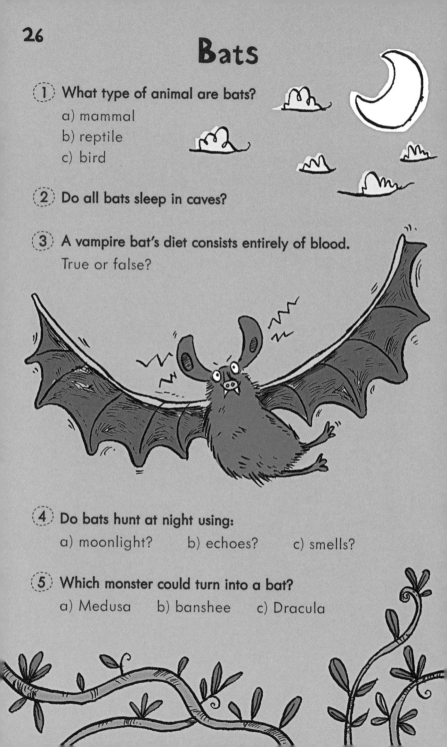

1. What type of animal are bats?
   a) mammal
   b) reptile
   c) bird

2. Do all bats sleep in caves?

3. A vampire bat's diet consists entirely of blood.
   True or false?

4. Do bats hunt at night using:
   a) moonlight?   b) echoes?   c) smells?

5. Which monster could turn into a bat?
   a) Medusa   b) banshee   c) Dracula

6 What is a baby bat called?
   a) pup
   b) chick
   c) kitten

7 What is a bat's screech as loud as?
   a) hand-clap
   b) dog's bark
   c) car horn

8 What percentage of the world's mammal species are bats?
   a) 5%   b) 10%   c) 20%

9 The world's largest bat is the size of which bird?
   a) robin   b) seagull   c) vulture

10 What has bat dung been used to make?
   a) gunpowder
   b) cement
   c) perfume

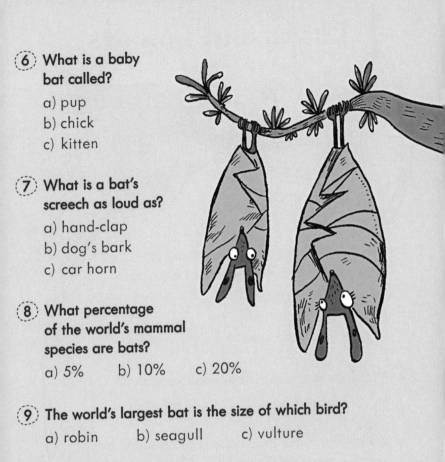

27

Leaps and bounds

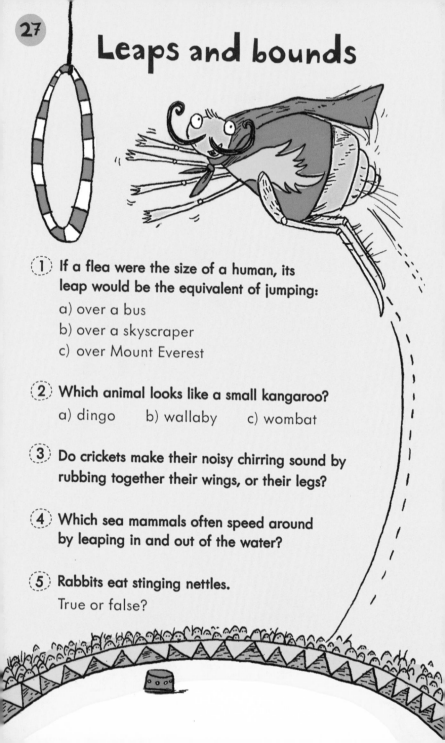

1. If a flea were the size of a human, its leap would be the equivalent of jumping:
   a) over a bus
   b) over a skyscraper
   c) over Mount Everest

2. Which animal looks like a small kangaroo?
   a) dingo   b) wallaby   c) wombat

3. Do crickets make their noisy chirring sound by rubbing together their wings, or their legs?

4. Which sea mammals often speed around by leaping in and out of the water?

5. Rabbits eat stinging nettles.
   True or false?

6 What is the name of this desert animal that has huge ears and hops like a kangaroo?

a) prairie dog
b) hamster
c) jerboa

7 What is a baby hare called?

a) leveret
b) harekin
c) kitten

8 Which is hairless at birth, a hare or a rabbit?

9 Up in the trees, how big a gap can lar gibbons swing across?

a) a car length
b) a bus length
c) a plane length

10 Can kangaroos hop backwards?

28

Whales and dolphins

1. A blue whale can blow its spout as high as a:
   a) 1-floor building
   b) 3-floor building
   c) 6-floor building

2. Is a killer whale really a whale?

3. Which animal has a 3m (10ft) horn on the middle of its head?
   a) beluga whale
   b) bowhead whale
   c) narwhal

4. Do dolphins have bellybuttons?

5. How many balloons could a blue whale blow up with one breath?
   a) 30   b) 500   c) 2,000

6 What is the name of the man in the Bible story who was swallowed by a whale?

a) Job   b) Jonah   c) Jeremiah

7 What do you call a group of dolphins?

a) pod   b) herd   c) shoal

8 What do dolphins drink?

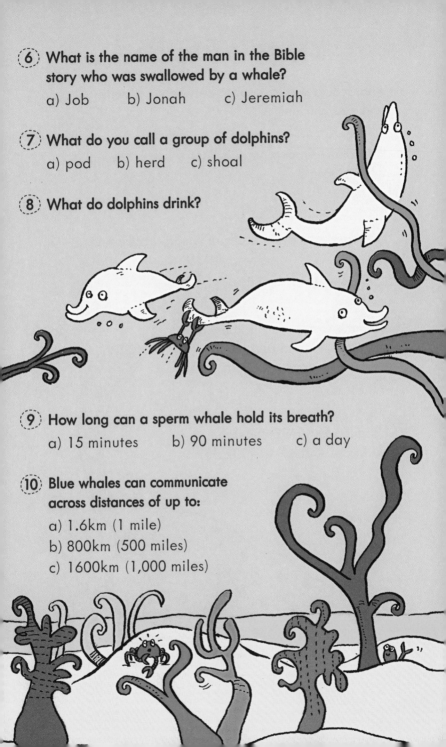

9 How long can a sperm whale hold its breath?

a) 15 minutes   b) 90 minutes   c) a day

10 Blue whales can communicate across distances of up to:

a) 1.6km (1 mile)
b) 800km (500 miles)
c) 1600km (1,000 miles)

Kings of speed

1. Who would win in a sprint between a gazelle and a horse?

2. How many times a second does a bee hummingbird flap its wings?
   a) 10   b) 80   c) 400

3. Put these animals in order of speed, fastest first.
   a) sloth   c) great white shark
   b) cheetah   d) spine-tailed swift

4. I am the fastest dog in the world.
   I am long-legged and thin.
   I sometimes race around a track.
   What am I?

5. How quickly can a cheetah go from 0-60mph (0-100kph)?
   a) 3 seconds
   b) 5 seconds
   c) 7 seconds

6 Which is the world's fastest snake?

   a) spitting cobra   b) black mamba   c) copperhead

7 How many times
a minute does a
mouse's heart beat?

   a) 200
   b) 500
   c) 1,000

8 Which bird is the fastest
animal that's ever lived?

   a) peregrine falcon
   b) buzzard
   c) swift

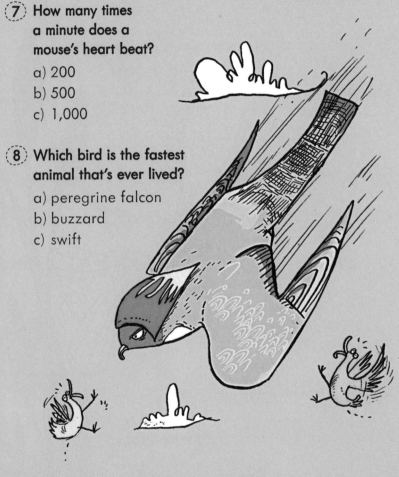

9 How long are bandicoots pregnant?

   a) 12 days   b) 30 days   c) 46 days

10 Which is the fastest fish on the planet?

   a) mackerel   b) barracuda   c) sailfish

30

True or false?

1. Any whales washed ashore in Britain belong to the Queen.

2. People ate cats in Ancient Rome.

3. Pigeons see in slow motion.

4. Penguins fly.

5. Dragonflies bite people.

6. Sharks are fish.

7. Hens have teeth.

8. Seagulls can breathe underwater.

9. Roadrunners are birds that run very fast.

10. Chimpanzees play 'baseball' with mangos.

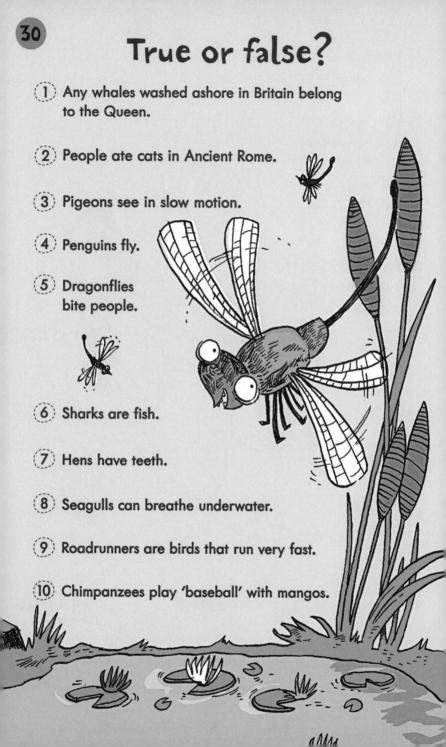

11) There's a fish that can climb trees to catch insects.

12) Bats always turn left when they leave a cave.

13) A walrus weighs more than a giraffe.

14) Jellyfish are 95% water.

15) Mice love cheese.

16) An elephant never forgets.

17) Unicorns lived up until the 14th century.

18) House flies vomit on all the food they land on.

19) A woodpecker listens for insects with its tongue.

20) Moles are blind.

31

Little animals

1. **What do caterpillars eat?**
   a) leaves
   b) slugs
   c) honey

2. **What's the name of the small rodent whose name rhymes with 'mole'?**

3. **Which animal lays eggs?**
   a) cat
   b) chameleon
   c) chipmunk

4. **Irukandji jellyfish are only 1cm (0.3in) wide, but their venom is stronger than a king cobra's. Is it:**
   a) 5 times as strong?
   b) 10 times as strong?
   c) 100 times as strong?

5. **What is the world's smallest breed of dog?**
   a) poodle   b) fox terrier   c) Chihuahua

6 How much of its life does a dormouse spend asleep?

a) 25%   b) 75%   c) 95%

7 Which mammal lives in the Egyptian pyramids?

a) tomb rat   b) tomb bat   c) tomb cat

8 What is the smallest spoon a newborn kangaroo could be picked up with?

a) teaspoon   b) soup spoon   c) ladle

9 What do tadpoles NOT grow into?

a) frogs
b) toads
c) moles

10 Which of these do hedgehogs eat?

a) snails
b) mice
c) grass

11 The nest a harvest mouse lives in is as small as a:

　a) grapefruit
　b) orange
　c) plum

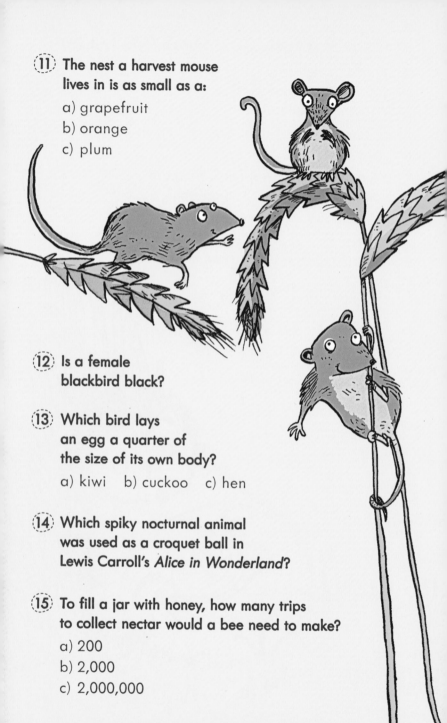

12 Is a female blackbird black?

13 Which bird lays an egg a quarter of the size of its own body?

　a) kiwi　b) cuckoo　c) hen

14 Which spiky nocturnal animal was used as a croquet ball in Lewis Carroll's *Alice in Wonderland*?

15 To fill a jar with honey, how many trips to collect nectar would a bee need to make?

　a) 200
　b) 2,000
　c) 2,000,000

Rainforest wildlife

1. Which is the most common rainforest mammal?

    a) monkey   b) squirrel   c) bat

2. One big meal is enough to keep a blood-sucking leech going for a year.
    True or false?

3. Which big cat lives in the Amazon rainforest?

    a) leopard   b) jaguar   c) tiger

4. In *The Jungle Book,* Mowgli was brought up by:

    a) wolves
    b) lions
    c) chimpanzees

5. What does 'orangutan' mean?

    a) man of the forest
    b) gentle giant
    c) the red spirit

6 A western lowland gorilla's scientific name is *Gorilla gorilla*.
True or false?

7 Do parrots build nests?

8 Which baby reptile squeaks inside its egg?
a) chameleon   b) alligator   c) cobra

9 Where do green mambas spend most of their time?
a) in water   b) in grass   c) in trees

10 What is the world's noisiest land animal?
a) howler monkey
b) screech owl
c) baboon

Animals in danger

1. **What most threatens rhinos' survival?**
   a) global warming
   b) poachers
   c) habitat loss

2. **What is a kakapo?**
   a) flightless parrot
   b) toothless crocodile
   c) furless mole

3. **In which country does the endangered Yangtze river dolphin live?**
   a) China   b) India   c) Russia

4. **Tasmanian tigers were leopard-sized carnivores that became extinct in the:**
   a) 10th century
   b) 15th century
   c) 20th century

5. **Where did dodos live before they became extinct?**
   a) New Zealand
   b) Galapagos Islands
   c) Mauritius

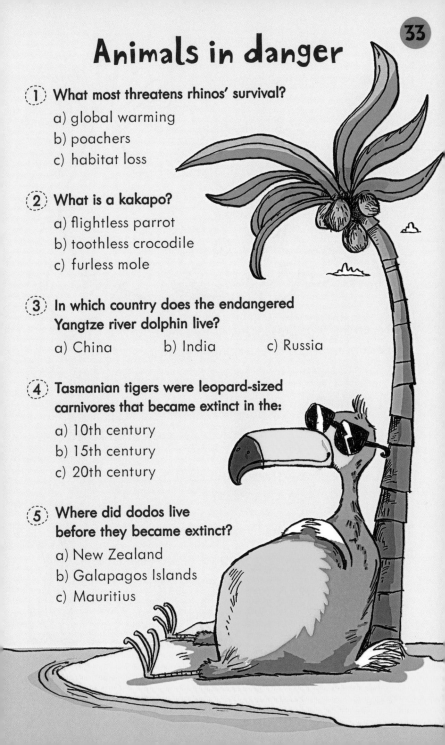

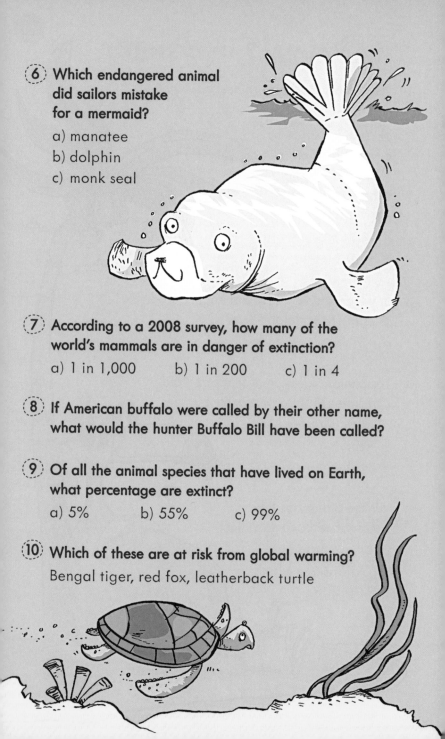

6) Which endangered animal did sailors mistake for a mermaid?
   a) manatee
   b) dolphin
   c) monk seal

7) According to a 2008 survey, how many of the world's mammals are in danger of extinction?
   a) 1 in 1,000   b) 1 in 200   c) 1 in 4

8) If American buffalo were called by their other name, what would the hunter Buffalo Bill have been called?

9) Of all the animal species that have lived on Earth, what percentage are extinct?
   a) 5%   b) 55%   c) 99%

10) Which of these are at risk from global warming?
   Bengal tiger, red fox, leatherback turtle

34

Slow and steady

1) What is a sloth's top speed?
   a) 0.25kph (0.15mph)
   b) 2.5kph (1.5mph)
   c) 25kph (15mph)

2) What plodding, big-eared animal is used to transport goods across rough terrain?

3) Where do pandas live?
   a) India   b) China   c) Philippines

4) Put these animals in the order they would finish a race, starting with last place.
   a) koala   b) sloth   c) snail   d) giant tortoise

5) Which of these is a real animal?
   a) slow worm   b) slow fish   c) slow snake

6 I have only one foot to move around on.
I have eyes on long, thin stalks.
I carry my home on my back.
What am I?

7 In the story of the hare and the tortoise, why did the hare lose the race?

a) he hurt his foot
b) he took a nap
c) he lost his way

8 What do koalas eat?

a) bamboo
b) pampas
c) eucalyptus

9 What is the record age for a giant tortoise?

a) 55 years old
b) 155 years old
c) 255 years old

10 Do slugs lay eggs?

35

Extreme tactics

1. How quickly can a king cobra's bite kill a human?

   a) 15 seconds   b) 15 minutes   c) 15 hours

2. Is the shock from an electric eel strong enough to kill you?

3. How do Malaysian ants defend their nest?

   a) biting
   b) spitting acid
   c) exploding

4. An octopus with a body the size of a bowling ball could squeeze through a hole the size of a:

   a) ping-pong ball   b) tennis ball   c) bowling ball

5. Which animal whirls its tail like a propeller to mark as much of its territory with dung as possible?

   a) hippo   b) warthog   c) Tasmanian devil

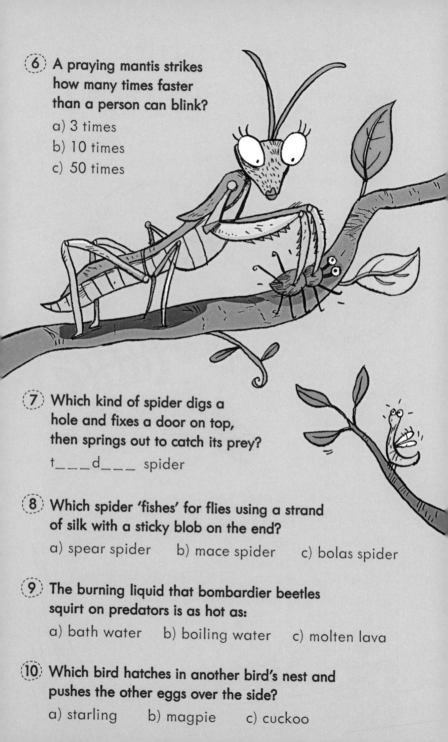

6 A praying mantis strikes how many times faster than a person can blink?
a) 3 times
b) 10 times
c) 50 times

7 Which kind of spider digs a hole and fixes a door on top, then springs out to catch its prey?

t_ _ _ d_ _ _ spider

8 Which spider 'fishes' for flies using a strand of silk with a sticky blob on the end?
a) spear spider   b) mace spider   c) bolas spider

9 The burning liquid that bombardier beetles squirt on predators is as hot as:
a) bath water   b) boiling water   c) molten lava

10 Which bird hatches in another bird's nest and pushes the other eggs over the side?
a) starling   b) magpie   c) cuckoo

36

Insects

(1) **Which of these is an insect?**

a) spider   b) centipede   c) butterfly

(2) **Which insects build structures four times as high as a person, with walls as tough as concrete?**

a) African honey bees   b) termites   c) ants

(3) **In the story of the ant and the grasshopper, what did the grasshopper ask the ant?**

a) to sail away in a pea-green boat
b) to lend him some food for winter
c) to bake him a custard tart

(4) **How do dung beetles get their name?**

a) they eat dung
b) they smell like dung
c) they live in dung

(5) **Why do bees dance?**

a) to show who's leader
b) to give directions to food
c) to warn of danger

(6) **Which of these is NOT a reason why fireflies glow?**

a) to attract a mate
b) to deter predators
c) to light their way

(7) **Do grasshoppers eat grass?**

(8) **Which statement about cockroaches is false?**

a) they could survive a nuclear war
b) they can survive for weeks without their head
c) they can live off the glue on the back of stamps

(9) **I am a large type of insect.**
I move in giant swarms that darken the sky.
I am a biblical plague.
What am I?

(10) **What's the common name for grubs that glow in the dark?**

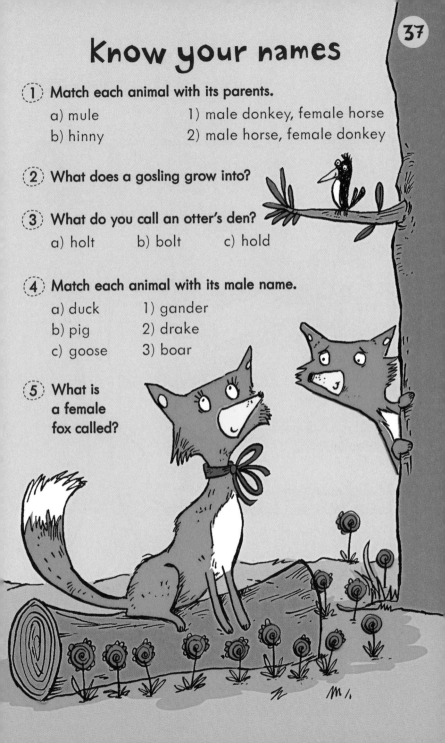

37

Know your names

1 Match each animal with its parents.

a) mule   1) male donkey, female horse

b) hinny   2) male horse, female donkey

2 What does a gosling grow into?

3 What do you call an otter's den?

a) holt   b) bolt   c) hold

4 Match each animal with its male name.

a) duck   1) gander

b) pig   2) drake

c) goose   3) boar

5 What is a female fox called?

6 Match each horse with its description.

a) colt   1) male horse
b) filly   2) newborn horse
c) mare   3) young female horse
d) stallion   4) young male horse
e) foal   5) female horse

7 What is a badger's den called?

8 Male donkeys are called Jacks. Are female donkeys called Jills or Jennies?

9 What is a baby goat called?
a) lamb   b) kid   c) fawn

10 What is the name for a female peacock?

38

Deep sea Creatures

1. Put these in order of how deep they live, deepest first.
   a) whale shark   b) seahorse   c) viper fish

2. Which is NOT the name of a deep-sea animal?
   a) vampire squid   b) goblin shark   c) troll fish

3. A colossal squid is longer than a bus.
   True or false?

4. Which fictional sea beast was hunted by Captain Ahab?
   a) Moby Dick   b) Hydra   c) Leviathan

5. At what depth have cusk eels been caught?
   a) 1.5km (1 mile)
   b) 8km (5 miles)
   c) 16km (10 miles)

6. Which fish lures its prey with a bright light?

7) Giant isopods crawl along ocean floors, and grow to the size of human babies. Which animal do they most resemble?

a) slug   b) woodlouse   c) millipede

8) What type of creature does the legendary sea-monster called the Kraken look most like?

a) great white shark
b) electric eel
c) giant squid

9) Would deep sea fish die if they were brought to the surface?

10) What is the name of this eel?

a) guzzler eel
b) gulper eel
c) greedy eel

39

Elephants

1. How many species of elephants are there?

   a) 1   b) 2   c) 3

2. An elephant drinks enough water each day to fill how many cola cans?

   a) 50   b) 200   c) 600

3. Which are bigger, Indian or African elephants?

4. Who marched over the Alps mountains with elephants in his army, to attack the Roman Empire?

   a) Alexander the Great
   b) Hannibal
   c) Genghis Khan

5. How many teeth do elephants use to chew their food?

   a) 4
   b) 32
   c) 56

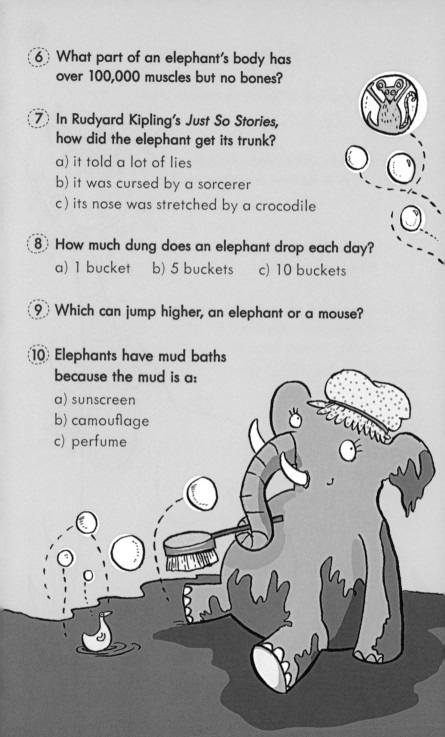

6) What part of an elephant's body has over 100,000 muscles but no bones?

7) In Rudyard Kipling's *Just So Stories*, how did the elephant get its trunk?
   a) it told a lot of lies
   b) it was cursed by a sorcerer
   c) its nose was stretched by a crocodile

8) How much dung does an elephant drop each day?
   a) 1 bucket   b) 5 buckets   c) 10 buckets

9) Which can jump higher, an elephant or a mouse?

10) Elephants have mud baths because the mud is a:
   a) sunscreen
   b) camouflage
   c) perfume

40

Animal all-sorts

1. **Which is the most common mammal on the planet?**
   a) rat   b) dog   c) human

2. **What does cold air give you?**
   a) goosebumps   b) dogbumps   c) bunnybumps

3. **Complete the film title:
   "101..."**
   a) Alsatians   b) Dalmatians   c) Crustaceans

4. **Do penguins swim by flapping their
   wings or kicking their feet?**

5. **Is a hyena's dung:**
   a) brown?
   b) white?
   c) red?

6) **Which Roman emperor wanted to make his horse a member of the government?**

a) Julius Caesar   b) Nero   c) Caligula

7) **Which insect has hairs growing out of its eyes?**

a) honeybee   b) moth   c) stick insect

8) **I was raised by apes in the jungle, and beat my chest as I swing through the trees. I have a wife named Jane.**

Who am I?

9) **Which animal are hippos most closely related to?**

a) rhino
b) whale
c) elephant

10) **Which cartoon animal says 'What's up, Doc?'**

a) Bugs Bunny   b) Daffy Duck   c) Mickey Mouse

11 Which animal sheds its outer skin all at once, leaving behind a 'sock' of dead skin?

    a) worm   b) slug   c) snake

12 Who is the famous golfer?

    a) Bear Woods   b) Tiger Woods   c) Eagle Woods

13 Tapeworms cling to human intestines. How long can they grow?

    a) 15mm (0.5in)   b) 15cm (6in)   c) 15m (50ft)

14 A zonkey is a cross between a zebra and a donkey. True or false?

15 How long can walrus tusks grow?

    a) 20cm (8in)
    b) 50cm (20in)
    c) 1m (40in)

41

Lakes and rivers

1. **Catfish get their name because they have:**
   a) furry skin   b) a bushy tail   c) long whiskers

2. **River eels swim thousands of miles across the ocean to spawn where?**
   a) Sargasso Sea   b) Red Sea   c) Caspian Sea

3. **I have the tail of a beaver, the bill of a duck and the feet of a large otter.** What am I?

4. **What's the name of the water rat in *The Wind in the Willows*?**

5. **What do you call a beaver's home?**
   a) den   b) fort   c) lodge

6) Do pike have teeth?

7) In which country is the legendary Loch Ness monster said to live?

a) Canada   b) Scotland   c) Norway

8) Do otters hunt during the day, at night, or both?

9) How does a beaver signal alarm?

a) gnaws down a tree
b) slaps the water with its tail
c) chatters its teeth

10) Do river kingfishers nest in trees or burrows?

No fishing

42

Right or wrong?

1. Wasps make honey.

2. In the Middle Ages, sheep were five times smaller than they are today.

3. Gandalf's horse is called Filofax.

4. Tasmanian Devils live in Tasmania.

5. One of the twelve animals in the Chinese zodiac is a penguin.

6. Caviar is made entirely from fish eggs.

7. Dogs are descended from wolves.

8. Parrots only mimic the language of the country where they were born.

9. Meerkats are a type of cat.

10. Clark Kent's secret identity is Batman.

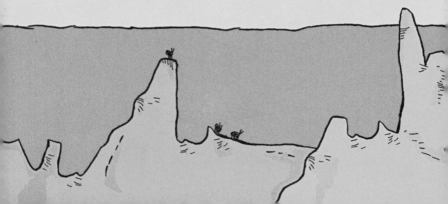

11. Coconut crabs crack open coconuts with their claws.

12. The dinosaur in *Toy Story* was named Rex.

13. Fermented herring is the smelliest man-made food.

14. Kingfishers were taught to fish for the King of England.

15. A chewbacca is a type of small Australian rodent.

16. In *The Wizard of Oz*, the lion asked for a brain.

17. Birds are the only living animals that are directly descended from dinosaurs.

18. An ostrich's eye is bigger than its brain.

19. A duck's quack doesn't echo.

20. Aardvarks eat 50,000 termites a night.

21. Arctic ice worms live in glaciers and melt in warm air.

22. The largest ever land mammal was a type of kangaroo.

23. Sloths are the only mammals that can't shiver.

24. Dolphins sometimes rescue drowning people.

25. A moose's antlers grow 2.5cm (1 inch) a day.

26. Hamsters always run clockwise around their wheel.

27. A bongo is a type of monkey.

28. There's a dragon on the Welsh flag.

29. Cows have four stomachs.

30. Giraffes can go for longer without drinking than camels.

43

Animals with shells

1. How many legs do crabs walk on?

2. Snails can crawl across the blade of a knife without being cut.
   True or false?

3. Which of these statements about lobsters is false?
   a) they were once fed mainly to slaves
   b) they scream when chefs boil them alive
   c) they can live for over 100 years

4. Inside which animal's shell are pearls found?
   a) winkle   b) conch   c) oyster

5. An African giant snail would cover your entire:
   a) hand
   b) face
   c) body

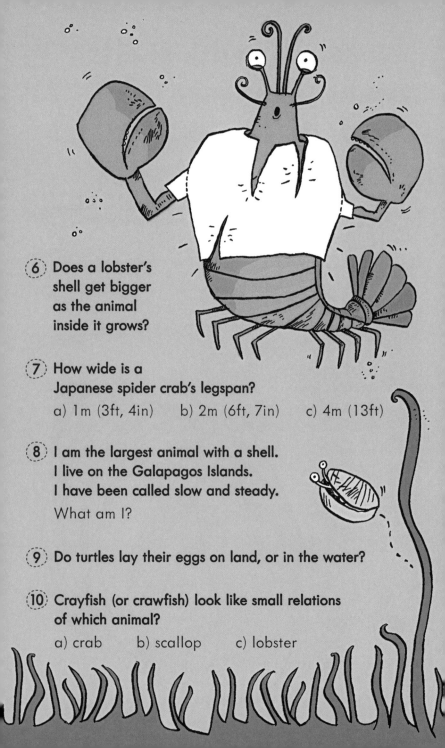

6) Does a lobster's shell get bigger as the animal inside it grows?

7) How wide is a Japanese spider crab's legspan?
a) 1m (3ft, 4in)   b) 2m (6ft, 7in)   c) 4m (13ft)

8) I am the largest animal with a shell. I live on the Galapagos Islands. I have been called slow and steady.
What am I?

9) Do turtles lay their eggs on land, or in the water?

10) Crayfish (or crawfish) look like small relations of which animal?
a) crab   b) scallop   c) lobster

44

Birds

1. Which South American bird looks like an ostrich?

   a) rhea   b) kiwi   c) macaw

2. Which is the odd one out?

   a) flamingo   b) ostrich   c) emu

3. What is the name of the mythical bird that dies in a ball of flames and is reborn from the ashes?

4. Is a bald eagle bald?

5. How long can a wandering albatross go without landing?

   a) 10 days
   b) 10 weeks
   c) 10 years

6) **What kind of bird is shown in the cartoon on the right?**

7) **Which bird is said to have the intelligence of a 5 year-old child?**
   a) African grey parrot
   b) tawny owl
   c) pelican

8) **A flamingo chick is:**
   a) pink
   b) yellow
   c) white

9) **Were tailor birds given their name because they:**
   a) stitch little jackets to keep their eggs warm?
   b) stitch a nest using a rolled up leaf and spider silk?
   c) stitch a 'scarecrow' to scare other birds away?

10) **How long does it take to hard-boil an ostrich egg?**
    a) 20 minutes
    b) 1 hour
    c) 2 hours

45

Open plains

1. Which animal leaps up and down to show predators how energetic it's feeling?

   a) gazelle   b) zebra   c) wildebeest

2. What do ostriches eat?

   a) worms   b) fish   c) leaves and grass

3. Which African mammal is nicknamed 'black death'?

   a) rhino   b) leopard   c) cape buffalo

4. A rhino horn is made from ivory.

   True or false?

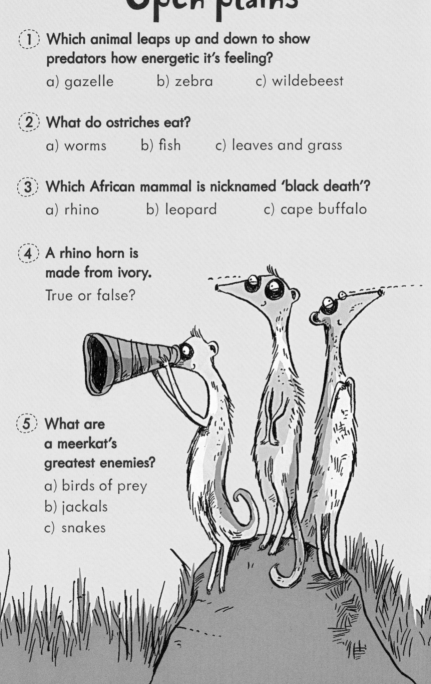

5. What are a meerkat's greatest enemies?

   a) birds of prey
   b) jackals
   c) snakes

6 Are zebras white with black stripes, or black with white stripes?

7 Where do armadillos live?
a) Australia
b) Africa
c) The Americas

8 Are hyenas more closely related to dogs or cats?

9 Which animal cleans its ears with its tongue?
a) giraffe
b) warthog
c) wildebeest

10 Which movie features a meerkat named Timon and a warthog named Pumbaa?

46

Kaleidoscope

1. Do small tropical creatures have bright markings to attract a mate, or to warn predators they're poisonous?

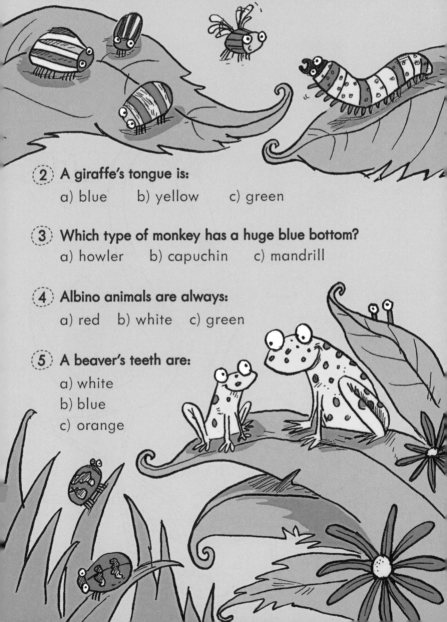

2. A giraffe's tongue is:
   a) blue   b) yellow   c) green

3. Which type of monkey has a huge blue bottom?
   a) howler   b) capuchin   c) mandrill

4. Albino animals are always:
   a) red   b) white   c) green

5. A beaver's teeth are:
   a) white
   b) blue
   c) orange

6) Which animal puts on light displays that slide across its skin like an electronic billboard?

a) catfish   b) cuttlefish   c) scorpion fish

7) Which bird's bill is blue, yellow and red?

a) canary   b) puffin   c) scarlet macaw

8) Flamingos feed their chicks:

a) pink milk
b) silver fish
c) green weeds

9) Is a black mamba snake:

a) silver
b) orange
c) black

10) Stripes are to a tiger as _ _ _ _ _ are to a cheetah.

47

Mountain animals

1. **What is the name of this mountain goat?**

   a) ibex   b) opec   c) inca

2. **I have a long neck, and I live in South America. My name begins with the same two letters.**

   What am I?

3. **What kind of animal does a pika look like?**

   a) lizard   b) goat   c) guinea pig

4. **Which bird is a national symbol for Russia and America?**

5. **What is the name of the rare leopard that lives high up in the Asian mountains?**

   a) ice leopard
   b) snow leopard
   c) mountain leopard

6 Which animal is often called a mountain lion?
   a) coyote   b) jackal   c) cougar

7 Which word goes before snowman to make the nickname of the legendary half-man half-ape creature that is said to live in the Himalayas?
   a) abominable   b) despicable   c) abysmal

8 Which of these animals is least likely to survive in snowy conditions?
   a) mouse   b) snake   c) bat

9 What are South American vultures called?

10 Where do yaks live?
   a) Himalayas
   b) Andes
   c) Rockies

Answers

1 **Big cats** 1. lion 2. c 3. a 4. mane 5. b 6. L, J (jaguars kill prey by biting through the skull) 7. true 8. tiger 9. c 10. lion

2 **Definitely deadly** 1. c 2. c 3. b 4. hyena (its call sounds like snatches of hysterical laughter) 5. b 6. a 7. piranha 8. a 9. c 10. a 11. b 12. mosquito (it carries deadly diseases) 13. tiger 14. b 15. a (rhinos follow their ears more than their eyes)

3 **Sharks** 1. c 2. a 3. killer whale (it's much bigger and more intelligent) 4. b 5. hammerhead shark 6. c (many are killed for shark fin soup; others get caught up in fishing nets) 7. b 8. a 9. b (it's a whale shark) 10. a

4 **Forest dwellers** 1. a (followed by Russia) 2. skunk 3. c 4. a 5. yes 6. a 7. b 8. beaver 9. b 10. a 11. wolf-dog cross 12. yes (but they much prefer to eat the baby bees) 13. c 14. they're all types of deer 15. c

5 **Pets** 1. yes 2. b (cats are more adaptable than dogs, because they don't need as much attention or space) 3. b (Carrots should only be given as a treat, because they contains lots of sugar. Also, rabbits should only eat lettuce that's dark green, because other types can be bad for them.) 4. c 5. true 6. hamster 7. a (she was the first dog to orbit the Earth, and died of overheating during the spaceflight) 8. c 9. a 10. b 11. c (if it fell dead off its perch, the miners knew there was a gas leak) 12. no (it's three months) 13. a 14. to warn other rabbits of danger 15. b

6 **Monkeys and apes** 1. b 2. c 3. b 4. a 5. false (Barbary macaques live in Gibraltar) 6. monkeys have tails 7. a 8. c 9. b (he flew the spaceship by pulling levers when they lit up) 10. b

7 **Animal giants** 1. c 2. blue whale 3. b 4. c 5. Godzilla 6. c 7. good luck 8. true 9. b 10. c 11. a 12. b 13. a 14. no 15. a d b c

8 **Birds of prey** 1. females 2. owl 3. a 4. eyrie 5. b 6. scavengers (they look for dead animals to eat) 7. b (it's a seabird) 8. a 9. b 10. a (bald eagles live in North America, and harpy eagles live in Central and South America)

9 **Creepy-crawlies** 1. b 2. centipedes 3. a 4. scorpion 5. b 6. yes 7. c 8. a 9. no 10. c 11. c (they eat bats!) 12. no (although sometimes they fall down the drain and get stuck) 13. false (some have more, some have fewer) 14. false 15. no (but one half may survive)

10 **Yes or no?** 1. yes (to sleep in) 2. yes 3. no (it can't swallow anything larger than a grapefruit) 4. yes 5. no (they only fly one way – home) 6. no (they have the same number) 7. yes (most animals can't) 8. yes 9. no (only mammals sweat) 10. yes 11. no (slow worms are legless lizards) 12. yes 13. no 14. no 15. no 16. yes (the most common species do) 17. no (but the larvae of some species do) 18. no 19. no (but they can see in very dim light) 20. yes

11 **On the farm** 1. a 2. b 3. true 4. breeds of cattle 5. a 6. b 7. c 8. no 9. billy goat 10. c

12 Snakes 1. a 2. b 3. polar regions 4. c 5. yes (lots) 6. a
7. b 8. Ireland 9. c (it lives in the Australian outback and
very rarely comes into contact with people) 10. no (snakes
don't have ears)

13 Fish 1. pike (it's the only one that doesn't live in the sea)
2. b 3. a 4. no (fish have backbones) 5. c 6. b 7. a
8. true (it goes into a trance) 9. true 10. c

14 Bears 1. c 2. b 3. no 4. in the night sky (they're
star constellations) 5. a 6. a 7. c 8. false 9. c 10. a
11. grizzly bears (they can break a lion's skull with one
swipe) 12. a (penguins live near the South Pole and polar
bears live near the North Pole) 13. b 14. c 15. a

15 The seasons 1. 'v' 2. c (except the queen, who
hibernates and starts a new colony in spring) 3. 'Show on
Earth' 4. ermine 5. a (some moths spin cocoons; butterflies
don't) 6. no (they have no winter) 7. b 8. a (it turns white)
9. no 10. separately

16 In the desert 1. Bactrian (Dromedaries have one hump)
2. c 3. a 4. false (dust devils are desert whirlwinds) 5. b
6. c 7. a 8. b 9. a 10. tail

17 Defensive trickery 1. a (puffer fish also inflate themselves,
but they don't have spines) 2. a 3. c (it has vivid markings
to show predators it's poisonous) 4. to avoid being eaten
by their parents 5. c (the tail continues squirming to be even
more distracting) 6. possum 7. camels 8. eyed 9. b 10. a

18 Down under 1. marsupials **2.** Tasmanian devil **3.** c **4.** a **5.** a **6.** c **7.** burrows **8.** b **9.** b **10.** false (30% live in the Americas)

19 Myth or fact? 1. myth **2.** fact **3.** myth **4.** fact (tears are forced out when they chew) **5.** fact **6.** myth **7.** myth (they store fat there) **8.** fact **9.** myth **10.** fact (and the nests themselves are made from bird spit) **11.** fact (they need a tiny bit of the central body, as well) **12.** myth (but they do have a high tolerance to it) **13.** fact **14.** myth **15.** fact **16.** myth (they see in blue and green) **17.** myth (it's background noise trapped inside the shell) **18.** myth **19.** myth **20.** fact

20 Seashore 1. crabs, starfish, limpets **2.** c **3.** black **4.** b **5.** hermit crab **6.** a **7.** Portuguese man o' war **8.** starfish **9.** b **10.** a

21 Rodents 1. b **2.** c (in the *Alvin and the Chipmunks* cartoon) **3.** c (they fall slowly because they're so light) **4.** no **5.** c **6.** b (the fleas came from China and crossed the Mediterranean Sea on rats aboard merchant ships) **7.** a **8.** rats **9.** a **10.** no

22 Ends of the Earth 1. a **2.** walrus **3.** South Pole **4.** c **5.** c **6.** c **7.** Dasher, Comet, Blitzen **8.** yes **9.** snow leopard **10.** b

23 Lizards 1. c (it's 3m (10ft) long) **2.** true **3.** chameleon **4.** b **5.** b **6.** c **7.** a **8.** b (snakes have no ears) **9.** cold blooded **10.** c

24 Frogs and toads 1. b **2.** c **3.** a **4.** b **5.** r (horror frog) **6.** yes (but toads don't) **7.** c **8.** a **9.** b **10.** false

25 After dark 1. a2, b1 (the male calls tu-whoo, the female answers tu-whit) **2.** red fox **3.** moth **4.** no **5.** b **6.** nightingale **7.** a **8.** tiger (spelled tyger in the poem) **9.** false **10.** tarsier

26 Bats 1. a **2.** no (some sleep in trees) **3.** true **4.** b **5.** c **6.** a **7.** c (but it's too high-pitched for humans to hear) **8.** c **9.** b (it's called a golden-capped fruit bat) **10.** a

27 Leaps and bounds 1. b **2.** b **3.** wings **4.** dolphins (or porpoises) **5.** true **6.** c **7.** a **8.** rabbit **9.** b **10.** no

28 Whales and dolphins 1. b **2.** no (it's a dolphin) **3.** c **4.** yes (all mammals have bellybuttons) **5.** c **6.** b **7.** a **8.** nothing (they survive on the water they get in their food) **9.** b **10.** c

29 Kings of speed 1. gazelle **2.** b **3.** d, b, c, a **4.** greyhound **5.** a (it can reach 70mph (110kph)) **6.** b **7.** b **8.** a (they reach 320kph (200mph) when diving after prey) **9.** a (it's the fastest pregnancy of any animal) **10.** c

30 True or false? 1. true **2.** false **3.** true **4.** false **5.** false **6.** true **7.** false **8.** false **9.** true **10.** false **11.** true (it's called a climbing perch) **12.** false **13.** true **14.** true **15.** false (they prefer chocolate) **16.** true (they can recognize an elephant they haven't seen for fifty years) **17.** false (they are legendary animals) **18.** false (they spit on it) **19.** true (insects make tiny vibrations in the wood that travel up the tongue to the bird's ear) **20.** false

31 Little animals 1. a **2.** vole **3.** b **4.** c **5.** c **6.** b **7.** b **8.** a **9.** c **10.** a **11.** c **12.** no (it's brown) **13.** a **14.** hedgehog **15.** c

32 **Rainforest wildlife** 1. c 2. true 3. b 4. a 5. a 6. false (it's *Gorilla gorilla gorilla*!) 7. no 8. b 9. c 10. a

33 **Animals in danger** 1. b 2. a 3. a 4. c (the last known Tasmanian tiger died in 1936) 5. c 6. a 7. c 8. Bison Bill 9. c 10. Bengal tiger and leatherback turtle

34 **Slow and steady** 1. a 2. donkey or mule 3. b 4. c, b, d, a 5. a (it's a legless lizard) 6. snail 7. b 8. c 9. c 10. yes

35 **Extreme tactics** 1. b 2. yes 3. c (they blow themselves up to cover predators in toxic glue) 4. a (they have no bones) 5. a 6. b (it's so fast it inspired a form of martial art) 7. trapdoor spider 8. c 9. b 10. c

36 **Insects** 1. c (insects have six legs) 2. b 3. b (he'd spent the summer playing rather than storing up food) 4. a 5. b 6. c 7. yes 8. a (they're actually less likely to survive than some other insects) 9. locust 10. glowworms

37 **Know your names** 1. a1, b2 2. goose 3. a 4. a2, b3, c1 5. vixen 6. a4, b3, c5, d1, e2 7. sett 8. Jennies 9. b 10. peahen

38 **Deep sea creatures** 1. c, a, b 2. c 3. true 4. a 5. b 6. angler fish 7. b 8. c 9. yes (their bodies aren't suited to the low-pressure conditions closer to the surface) 10. b

39 **Elephants** 1. c (African bush, African forest, Indian) 2. c 3. African 4. b 5. a 6. its trunk 7. c 8. b 9. mouse (elephants can't jump) 10. a

40 **Animal all-sorts** 1. a 2. a 3. b 4. flapping their wings 5. b (because of all the bones it eats) 6. c 7. a (they protect the eye by trapping dust and pollen) 8. Tarzan 9. b 10. a 11. c 12. b 13. c 14. true (it's also known as a zedonk) 15. c

41 **Lakes and rivers** 1. c 2. a 3. platypus 4. Ratty 5. c 6. yes 7. b 8. both 9. b 10. burrows

42 **Right or wrong?** 1. wrong 2. right (they've since been bred to increase their size so they produce more wool and meat) 3. wrong (it's called Shadowfax) 4. right 5. wrong 6. right 7. right 8. wrong 9. wrong 10. wrong (it's Superman) 11. right 12. right 13. right (it's called surströmming, and open barrels of it are said to have knocked seagulls unconscious) 14. wrong 15. wrong (it's a character in the *Star Wars* films) 16. wrong (he asked for courage) 17. right 18. right 19. wrong 20. right 21. right 22. wrong (it was a type of rhino) 23. right 24. right (they've lifted drowning people to the surface, or helped them swim to shore) 25. right (they're the fastest growing animal part) 26. wrong 27. wrong (it's a type of antelope) 28. right 29. wrong (they have one stomach split into four parts) 30. right

43 **Animals with shells** 1. 8 (but they have 10 in total because scientists also count their claws as legs) 2. true 3. b (the 'scream' is air escaping from the shell) 4. c 5. b 6. no (it discards it and grows a bigger one) 7. c 8. giant tortoise 9. on land 10. c

44 **Birds** 1. a 2. a (it's the only one that can fly) 3. phoenix 4. no (its head is covered in white feathers) 5. c (they spend most of their life gliding over the ocean) 6. toucan 7. a 8. c (flamingos only turn pink when they eat shrimp) 9. b 10. b

45 **Open plains** 1. a 2. c 3. c 4. false (it's made from the same stuff as your hair and nails) 5. a 6. black with white stripes (the white stripes are areas where the fur's natural pigmentation is absent) 7. c 8. cats 9. a 10. *The Lion King*

46 **Kaleidoscope** 1. to warn predators they're poisonous (or to pretend they are) 2. a 3. c 4. b 5. c 6. b 7. b 8. a 9. a 10. spots

47 **Mountain animals** 1. a 2. llama 3. c 4. eagle (the Russian symbol is a double-headed eagle, the American is a bald eagle) 5. b 6. c 7. a 8. b (they're cold blooded) 9. condors 10. a

With thanks to Michael Hill

First published in 2015 by Usborne Publishing Ltd, 83–85 Saffron Hill, London ECIN 8RT, England.
Copyright © 2015 Usborne Publishing Ltd. The name Usborne and the devices ♀♥ are Trade Marks of Usborne Publishing Ltd.
All rights reserved. No part of this publication may be reproduced, stored in a retrieval system, or transmitted in any form or by any means, mechanical, electronic, photocopying, recording or otherwise, without the prior permission of the publisher.
First published in America in 2017. AE.